Grant Us Peace

Revised Edition

LTP

LITURGY
TRAINING
PUBLICATIONS

ACKNOWLEDGMENTS

We are grateful to the many publishers and authors who have given permission to include their work. Every effort has been made to determine the ownership of all texts and to make proper arrangements for their use. We will gladly correct in future editions any oversight or error that is brought to our attention.

Scripture texts, unless otherwise noted, are from the *New Revised Standard Version Bible,* © 1989, Division of Christian Education of the National Council of the Churches of Christ in the United States of America. Used with permission. All rights reserved.

English translation of Psalms 22 and 85 from *The Psalms,* © 2000, The Grail (England).

Acknowledgments for specific texts, along with other information (e.g., suggestions for how the song texts can be sung) will be found on pages 54–57.

Texts and other suggestions for this book came from various persons at Liturgy Training Publications and Pax Christi; the concept for the book was suggested by John Wright.

[acknowledgments continued on page 54]

GRANT US PEACE copyright © 1991, 2002 Archdiocese of Chicago: Liturgy Training Publications, 1800 North Hermitage Avenue, Chicago IL 60622-1101; 1-800-933-1800, fax 1-800-933-7094, e-mail orders@ltp.org. All rights reserved. See our website at www.ltp.org.

This book was edited by Gabe Huck, Vicky Tufano and Lorie Simmons. Carol Mycio was the production editor. The cover design is by Anne Fritzinger and the interior is based on a design by Anna Manhart. Typesetting was done by Anne Fritzinger in Galliard. Cover image is by ArtToday © 2002 www.arttoday.com. The interior art is by Jane Pitz. Printed by ABS Graphics, Inc., in Addison, Illinois.

Library of Congress Control Number: 2002141200

1-56854-441-3

PEACE2

CONTENTS

FOREWORD TO THE SECOND EDITION

On September 11, 2001, and for days after, the world stood transfixed and horrified by images of the World Trade Center towers and the Pentagon engulfed in flames. Thousands died that day. Millions more felt helpless. People of faith turned to prayer.

We at LTP offer this small book at yet another time of sadness and death, when churches and individuals are seeking resources for prayer. It has been updated only slightly. The fine prayers, songs and reflections contained in the first edition continue to offer wisdom, comfort and challenge.

—*Vicky Tufano, 2001*

FOREWORD TO THE FIRST EDITION

This book exists as a reminder and a resource. It is to remind us that what we call justice and what we call peace are thoroughly woven into Christian discourse. We do not pray or proclaim scripture without the images for justice and for peace given to us by our ancestors and our contemporaries. Many of these texts we know already. They are on these pages to give them new life on our lips: that they might do their work and make just persons and peacemakers of those who would, day by day, speak such words. They give us a world and a task.

As a resource, this book offers texts that may be used when people assemble to pray for peace and for justice. The texts were gathered in January of 1991 as the United States began a war against Iraq. Those weeks made it clear that churches and individuals were asking for a resource like this.

When we decided to do this book, I approached Pax Christi to see if we could assist each other through its publication. A number of the texts here come from their materials and a portion of our income from the sale of *Grant Us Peace* will go to Pax Christi. Those who use this book might well consider learning about and perhaps joining Pax Christi USA. They can be contacted at 532 West Eighth Street, Erie, PA 16502; 814-453-4955; info@paxchristiusa.org.

—*Gabe Huck, 1991*

TABLE PRAYERS

Before taking food, we give thanks and intercede
for our world.

All the world hopes in you, O Lord,
that you will give us food in our hunger.
You open wide your hand
and we are filled with good things.

Lord, the lover of life,
you feed the birds of the skies
and array the lilies of the field.
We bless you for all your creatures
and for the food we are about to receive.
We humbly pray that in your goodness
you will provide for our brothers and sisters
who are hungry.

We ask this through Christ our Lord.

After eating:

The poor shall eat and shall have their fill.
Those who long for the Lord shall give praise.

—*Catholic Household Blessings and Prayers*

MORNING

The first prayer is the sign of the cross. In this gesture we bind ourselves to the dying of Christ and to Christ's victory over evil.

Very early in the day we bind ourselves also to all the poor:

Blessed are you, Lord, God of all creation:
you raise up those who are bowed down.

Blessed are you, Lord, God of all creation:
you set captives free.

Blessed are you, Lord, God of all creation:
you clothe the naked.

  —*Adapted from* Gates of Prayer

*The church's morning canticle, the Song of Zachary,
praises God for the dawning of days that will bring
deliverance, justice, peace.*

Blessed are you, Lord, the God of Israel,
you have come to your people and set them free.
You have raised up for us a mighty Savior,
born of the house of your servant David.

In the tender compassion of our God
the dawn from on high shall break upon us,
to shine on those who dwell in darkness
    and the shadow of death,
and to guide our feet into the way of peace.

    —*Luke 1:68–69, 78–79*

*Along that "way of peace," we repeat every morning
the Lord's Prayer.*

Embracing the new day, we proclaim:

Peace before us, peace behind us, peace under our feet.
Peace within us, peace over us,
let all around us be peace.

    —*Based on a Navajo Prayer*

MIDDAY

May the peace of God that is beyond all
understanding guard our hearts and our thoughts
in Christ Jesus.

   —*From Philippians 4:7*

God of the humble and helper of the oppressed:
Blessed are you, Lord!
Supporter of the weak and refuge of the forsaken:
Blessed are you, Lord!

   —*From Judith 9:11*

EVENING

*As we move from the time of light into the time of
darkness, the church prays for the world and for the
coming of God's reign.*

In peace, we pray to the Lord.

For an evening that is perfect, holy, peaceful and
without sin, let us pray:

Lord, have mercy.

For the peace of the world, that a spirit of respect and forbearance may grow among nations and peoples, let us pray:

Lord, have mercy.

For those in positions of public trust, (especially _____), that they may serve justice and promote the dignity and freedom of all people, let us pray:

Lord, have mercy.

For this city and for every city and country, and for all those living in them, let us pray:

Lord, have mercy.

For seasonable weather, for bountiful harvests and for peaceful times, let us pray:

Lord, have mercy.

For the poor, the persecuted, the sick and all who suffer; for refugees, prisoners and all who are in danger, that they may be relieved and protected, let us pray:

Lord, have mercy.

For our enemies and those who wish us harm,
and for all whom we have injured or offended,
let us pray:

Lord, have mercy.

For a peaceful and Christian end to our lives,
let us pray:

Lord, have mercy.

—*Ancient Christian Litany*

*The church's evening canticle, the Song of Mary,
proclaims God's own justice.*

My soul proclaims the greatness of the Lord,
my spirit rejoices in God my Savior,
for you, Lord, have looked with favor
    on your lowly servant.

You have shown strength with your arm
and scattered the proud in their conceit,
casting down the mighty from their thrones
and lifting up the lowly.
You have filled the hungry with good things
and sent the rich away empty.

You have come to the aid of your servant Israel,
to remember the promise of mercy,
the promise made to our forebears,
to Abraham and his children for ever.

—Luke 2:47–48, 51–55

NIGHT

May the all-powerful Lord grant us a restful night
and a peaceful death.

Protect us, Lord, as we stay awake;
watch over us as we sleep,
that awake, we may keep watch with Christ,
and asleep, rest in his peace.

The day ends as it began, with the sign of the cross.

Lord, bless this household and each one.
Place the cross of Christ on us
    with the power of your love
until we see the land of joy.

—Catholic Household Blessings and Prayers

SUNDAY

*Sunday is the Lord's Day. It is the day when Christians
have anticipated in exile the coming of God's reign.
At the heart of our Sunday is our gathering to listen
to the scriptures and to celebrate the eucharist. The
words we hear and speak at this assembly are worthy
of repetition at other moments on Sunday and
throughout the week.*

The peace of the Lord be with you always.

Lamb of God, you take away the sins of the world:
grant us peace.

Lord, may this sacrifice,
which has made our peace with you,
advance the peace and salvation of all the world.
Remember those who have died in the peace of Christ
and all the dead whose faith is known to you alone.

Lord Jesus Christ, you said to your apostles:
I leave you peace, my peace I give you.
Look not on our sins, but on the faith
    of your Church,
and grant us the peace and unity of your kingdom
where you live for ever and ever.

In the midst of conflict and division,
we know it is you
who turn our minds to thoughts of peace.
Your Spirit changes our hearts:
enemies begin to speak to one another,
those who were estranged join hands in friendship,
and nations seek the way of peace together.

Your Spirit is at work
when understanding puts an end to strife,
when hatred is quenched by mercy,
and vengeance gives way to forgiveness.

In that new world where the fullness of your peace
    will be revealed,
gather people of every race, language, and way of life
to share in the one eternal banquet
with Jesus Christ the Lord.

Deliver us, Lord, from every evil, and grant us peace
in our day. In your mercy keep us free from sin and
protect us from all anxiety as we wait in joyful hope
for the coming of our Savior, Jesus Christ.

—*The Roman Missal*

FRIDAY

As a tangible sign of our need and desire to do penance we, for the cause of peace, commit ourselves to fast, and abstinence on each Friday of the year. We call upon our people voluntarily to do penance on Friday by eating less food and by abstaining from meat. This return to a traditional practice of penance, once well observed in the U.S. Church, should be accompanied by works of charity and service toward our neighbors. Every Friday should be a day significantly devoted to prayer, penance, and almsgiving for peace.

—*U.S. Catholic Bishops,* The Challenge of Peace

Is not this the fast that I choose:
    to loose the bonds of injustice,
    to undo the thongs of the yoke,
to let the oppressed go free,
    and to break every yoke?
Is it not to share your bread with the hungry,
    and bring the homeless poor into your house?

—*Isaiah 58:6–7*

All praise be yours, God our Creator,
as we wait in joyful hope
for the flowering of justice
and the fullness of peace.
All praise for this day, this Friday.
By our weekly fasting and prayer,
cast out the spirit of war, of fear and mistrust,
and make us grow hungry for human kindness,
thirsty for solidarity with all the people
   of your dear earth.
May all our prayer, our fasting and our deeds
be done in the name of Jesus.

   —*Gabe Huck*

When giving or receiving alms:

May God fully supply all our needs.

   —*From Philippians 4:19*

ADVENT

God of majesty and power,
amid the clamour of our violence
your Word of truth resounds;
upon a world made dark by sin
the Sun of Justice casts his dawning rays.

Keep your household watchful
and aware of the hour in which we live.
Hasten the advent of that day
when the sounds of war will be for ever stilled,
the darkness of evil scattered,
and all your children gathered into one.

We ask this through him whose coming is certain,
whose day draws near:
your Son, our Lord Jesus Christ,
who lives and reigns with you in the unity
    of the Holy Spirit,
God for ever and ever.

    —Opening Prayers

I will hear what the LORD has to say,
a voice that speaks of peace,
peace for his people and friends
and those who turn to God in their hearts.
Salvation is near for the God-fearing,
and his glory will dwell in our land.
Mercy and faithfulness have met;
justice and peace have embraced.
Faithfulness shall spring from the earth
and justice look down from heaven.

The LORD will make us prosper
and our earth shall yield its fruit.
Justice shall march to the forefront,
and peace shall follow the way.

—*Psalm 85:9–14*

O come, Desire of nations, bind
In one the hearts of humankind;
O bid our sad divisions cease,
And be for us our King of Peace.

—*From O Come, O Come, Emmanuel*

CHRISTMAS SEASON

The people who walked in darkness
    have seen a great light;
those who lived in a land of deep darkness—
    on them light has shined.
For the yoke of their burden,
    and the bar across their shoulders,
    the rod of their oppressor,
    you have broken as on the day of Midian.
For all the boots of the tramping warriors
    and all the garments rolled in blood
    shall be burned as fuel for the fire.

    —*Isaiah 9:2–3, 4–5*

God of shepherds and all the poor,
God of magi and all who wander,
make bright this year's long night
with a bonfire of battle gear.
Make this season loud with the joyful sound
of every kind of weapon
being beaten, beaten, beaten
into the kind tools of common people.
Then with every creature
shall we sing the angels' song of glory and of peace.

    —*Gabe Huck*

Yet with the woes of sin and strife,
The world has suffered long;
Beneath the heav'nly hymn have rolled
Two thousand years of wrong;
And warring humankind hears not
The tidings which they bring;
O hush the noise and cease your strife
And hear the angels sing.

For, lo, the days are hastening on,
By prophets seen of old,
When with the ever circling years
Shall come the time foretold,
When peace shall over all the earth
Its ancient splendors fling,
And all the world give back the song
Which now the angels sing.

—*Edmund Hamilton Sears*

LENT

Again we keep this solemn fast,
A gift of faith from ages past,
This Lent which binds us lovingly
To faith and hope and charity.

More sparing, therefore, let us make
The words we speak, the food we take,
Our speech, our laughter, ev'ry sense;
Learn peace through holy penitence.

—Ancient Lenten Hymn

Merciful God,
you called us forth from the dust of the earth;
you claimed us for Christ in the waters of baptism.
Look upon us as we enter these Forty Days,
bearing the mark of ashes,
and bless our journey through the desert of Lent
to the font of rebirth.
May our fasting be hunger for justice;
our alms, a making of peace;
our prayer, the chant of humble and grateful hearts.
All that we do and pray is in the name of Jesus,
for in his cross you proclaim your love
for ever and ever.

—Catholic Household Blessings and Prayers

Rise up, O LORD; O God, lift up your hand;
    do not forget the oppressed.
Why do the wicked renounce God,
    and say in their hearts, "You will not call us
        to account"?
But you do see! Indeed you note trouble and grief,
    that you may take it into your hands;
the helpless commit themselves to you;
    you have been the helper of the orphan.

O LORD, you will hear the desire of the meek;
    you will strengthen their heart,
        you will incline your ear
to do justice for the orphan and the oppressed,
    so that those from earth may strike terror
        no more.

    —*Psalm 10:12–14, 17–18*

Paschal Triduum

We should glory in the cross of our Lord Jesus Christ, for he is our salvation, our life and our resurrection; through him we are saved and made free.

—*Holy Thursday Liturgy, from Galatians 6:14*

Ubi caritas et amor,
Deus ibi est.

Where charity and love are found,
there is God.

—*Antiphon, Preparation of the Gifts, Holy Thursday*
  Mass of the Lord's Supper

Like water I am poured out,
disjointed are all my bones.
My heart has become like wax,
it is melted within my breast.
Parched as burnt clay is my throat,
my tongue cleaves to my jaws.

God has never despised
nor scorned the poverty of the poor,
nor looked away from them,
but has heard the poor when they cried.

The poor shall eat and have their fill.
Those who seek the LORD shall praise the LORD.
May their hearts live for ever and ever!

   —*Psalm 22:15–16, 25, 27*

O God of unchangeable power and eternal light, let
the whole world see and know that things which
were cast down are being raised up, and things which
had grown old are being made new, and that all
things are being brought to their perfection by him
through whom all things were made, your Son
Jesus Christ our Lord.

   —*Book of Common Prayer*

Will you proclaim by word and example
   the Good News of God in Christ?
Will you seek and serve Christ in all persons,
   loving your neighbor as yourself?
Will you strive for justice and peace among all people,
   and respect the dignity of every human being?

   —*Book of Common Prayer*

Easter Season

Peace be with you.

—John 20:19

I am about to create new heavens
    and a new earth;
the former things shall not be remembered
    or come to mind.
Be glad and rejoice forever
    in what I am creating;
for I am about to create Jerusalem as a joy,
    and its people as a delight.
I will rejoice in Jerusalem,
    and delight in my people;
no more shall the sound of weeping be heard in it,
    or the cry of distress.

—Isaiah 65:17–19

Love the dispossessed, all those who, living amid human injustice, thirst after justice. Jesus had a special concern for them. Have no fear of being disturbed by them.

—Rule of Taizé

Our struggle is not against enemies of blood and flesh, but against the rulers, against the authorities, against the cosmic powers of this present darkness, against the spiritual forces of evil in the heavenly places. Therefore take up the whole armor of God, so that you may be able to withstand on that evil day, and having done everything, to stand firm. Stand therefore, and fasten the belt of truth around your waist, and put on the breastplate of righteousness. As shoes for your feet put on whatever will make you ready to proclaim the gospel of peace.

—Ephesians 6:12–15

Come, O Father of the poor,
Come, whose treasured gifts endure,
Come, our heart's unfailing light!
Bend the stubborn heart and will,
Melt the frozen, warm the chill,
Guide the wayward home once more.

—From Sequence of Pentecost

FEASTS AND FASTS

January 1, New Year's Day

Lord, make me an instrument of your peace:
where there is hatred, let me sow love;
where there is injury, pardon;
where there is doubt, faith;
where there is despair, hope;
where there is darkness, light;
where there is sadness, joy.

O divine Master, grant that I may not so much seek
to be consoled as to console,
to be understood as to understand,
to be loved as to love.
For it is in giving that we receive,
it is in pardoning that we are pardoned,
it is in dying that we are born to eternal life.

—*Often called the Prayer of Saint Francis*

The circle of a girl's arms has changed the world,
the round, sorrowful world, to a cradle for God.
O Mother of God, be hands that are rocking the
world to a kind of rhythm of love: that the incoherence of war and the chaos of unrest be soothed to
a lullaby, and the round, sorrowful world, in your
hands, the cradle of God.

—*Caryll Houselander*

January 15, Birthday of Martin Luther King, Jr.

Lord our God,
see how oppression and violence are
    our sad inheritance,
one generation to the next.
We look for you where the lowly are raised up,
where the mighty are brought down.
We find you there in your servants,
and we give you thanks this day
for your preacher and witness, Martin Luther King, Jr.
Fill us with your spirit:
where our human community is divided by racism,
torn by repression,
saddened by fear and ignorance,
may we give ourselves to your work of healing.

—*Catholic Household Blessings and Prayers*

March 24, Anniversary of the Assassination of Oscar Romero

On this day in 1980, Oscar Romero, the archbishop of San Salvador, was assassinated as he presided at the eucharistic liturgy. These are words from his homilies:

The church's good name is not a matter of being on good terms with the powerful. The church's good name is a matter of knowing that the poor regard the church as their own, of knowing that the church's life on earth is to call on all, on the rich as well, to be converted and be saved alongside the poor, for they are the only ones called blessed.

The church, entrusted with the earth's glory, believes that in each person is the Creator's image and that everyone who tramples it offends God. As holy defender of God's rights and of God's images, the church must cry out. It takes as spittle in its face, as lashes on its back, as the cross in its passion, all that human beings suffer, even though they be unbelievers. They suffer as God's images. There is no dichotomy between the human person and God's image. Whoever tortures a human being, whoever abuses a human being, whoever outrages a human being abuses God's image, and the church takes as its own that cross, that martyrdom.

—*Oscar Romero*

Yom Hashoah, Holocaust Memorial Day

Twelve days after Passover, Jews remember and mourn the six million who perished in the Holocaust. Christians join in this observance with penitential prayer.

Exalted, compassionate God,
grant perfect peace in your sheltering Presence,
among the holy and the pure,
to the souls of all the men, women and children
of the house of Israel,
to the Righteous Gentiles,
to the millions who died at a time of madness
    and terror.
May their memory endure;
may it inspire truth and loyalty in our lives,
in our religious commitment and tasks.
May their memory be a blessing
and sign of peace for all humanity.
And let us say all together: Amen.

—*Gabe Huck*

July 4, Independence Day

God, source of all freedom,
this day is bright with the memory
of those who declared that life and liberty
are your gift to every human being.

Help us to continue a good work begun long ago.
Make our vision clear and our will strong:
that only in human solidarity will we find liberty,
and justice only in the honor that belongs
to every life on earth.

Turn our hearts toward the family of nations:
to understand the ways of others,
to offer friendship,
and to find safety only in the common good of all.

—*Catholic Household Blessings and Prayers*

August 6 and August 9, Hiroshima and Nagasaki

On these two days the world remembers the only use in war of nuclear weapons, the bombing of Hiroshima and Nagasaki in 1945.

After the passage of nearly four decades and a concomitant growth in our understanding of the ever-growing horror of nuclear war, we must shape the climate of opinion which will make it possible for our country to express profound sorrow over the atomic bombing in 1945. Without that sorrow, there is no possibility of finding a way to repudiate future use of nuclear weapons.

—*U.S. Catholic Bishops*, The Challenge of Peace

To remember Hiroshima is to abhor nuclear war. To remember what the people of that city suffered is to renew our faith in humanity, in our capacity to do what is good, in our freedom to choose what is right, in our determination to turn disaster into a new beginning. In the face of the . . . calamity that every war is, one must affirm and reaffirm, again and again, that the waging of war is not inevitable or unchangeable. Humanity is not destined to self-destruction.

—*John Paul II*

September 11, World Trade Center and Pentagon

On this day we remember those who died in the destruction of the World Trade Center in New York and the Pentagon in Washington, D.C., by three hijacked airplanes. We remember those who died attempting to rescue people from those buildings and those who died in the crash of a fourth hijacked airplane in Pennsylvania. We also remember all victims of terrorism.

The human heart has depths from which schemes of unheard-of ferocity sometimes emerge, capable of destroying in a moment the normal daily life of a people. But faith comes to our aid at these times when words seem to fail. Christ's word is the only one that can give a response to the questions which trouble our spirit. Even if the forces of darkness appear to prevail, those who believe in God know that evil and death do not have the final say. Christian hope is based on this truth; at this time our prayerful trust draws strength from it.

—*John Paul II*

We believe that the one God calls us to be peoples of peace. Nothing in our Holy Scriptures, nothing in our understanding of God's revelation, nothing that is Christian or Islamic justifies terrorist acts and disruption of millions of lives which we have witnessed this week. Together we condemn those actions as evil and diametrically opposed to true religion.

—*Joint statement of U.S. Catholic Bishops and North American Muslim Leaders*

October 4, Saint Francis of Assisi

Francis lived in the thirteenth century; he practiced and taught a way of peace and of solidarity with the poor. These are words from his poem of praise to God:

Be praised, my Lord, with all your creatures,
Especially Brother Sun,
By whom you give us the light of day!
Be praised, my Lord, for Sister Moon and the Stars!
In the sky you formed them bright and lovely
    and fair.
Be praised, my Lord, for those who forgive
    for love of you
And endure infirmities and tribulations.
Blessed are those who shall endure these things
    in peace,
For by you, Most High, they will be crowned.

November 11, Saint Martin

Martin lived in the fourth century. Many consider him the patron of conscientious objectors. In 1963, the U.S. Bishops wrote in their pastoral letter, The Challenge of Peace:

Moved by the example of Jesus' life and by his teaching, some Christians have from the earliest days of the Church committed themselves to a non-violent lifestyle.* Some understood the gospel of Jesus to prohibit all killing. Some affirmed the use of prayer and other spiritual methods as a means of responding to enmity and hostility. . . . Some of the early Christian opposition to military service was a response to the idolatrous practices which prevailed in the Roman army. Another powerful motive was the fact that army service involved preparation for fighting and killing. We see this in the case of St. Martin of Tours during the fourth century, who renounced his soldierly profession with the explanation: "Hitherto I have served you as a soldier. Allow me now to become a soldier of God. . . . I am a soldier of Christ. It is not lawful for me to fight."*

*Martin's Day is a harvest festival in much of Europe.
The American Thanksgiving Day has its roots in such
festivals. Thanksgiving for the harvest and the
obligation to care for the poor, especially as winter
comes on, are always linked in our traditions.*

Thanksgiving Day

Lord, we thank you
for the goodness of our people
and for the spirit of justice
that fills this nation.
We thank you for the beauty and fullness of the
    land and the challenge of the cities.
We thank you for our work and our rest,
for one another, and for our homes.
We thank you, Lord:

For all that we have spoken
and for all that we keep in our hearts,
accept our thanksgiving on this day.

—*Catholic Household Blessings and Prayers*

November 29, Anniversary of the Death of Dorothy Day

Dorothy Day, cofounder of the Catholic Worker movement and houses of hospitality, died on this day in 1980. She wrote:

Can there be a just war? Can the conditions laid down by St. Thomas ever be fulfilled? What about the morality of the use of the atom bomb? What does God want me to do? And what am I capable of doing? Can I stand out against state and Church? Is it pride, presumption, to think I have the spiritual capacity to use spiritual weapons in the face of the most gigantic tyranny the world has ever seen? Am I capable of enduring suffering, facing martyrdom? And alone?

Again the long loneliness to be faced.

December 2, Anniversary of the Deaths of Four Church Women in El Salvador

Four women from the United States, who had been working with the poor of El Salvador, were murdered on this day in 1980. A few weeks before, one of them, Maura Clarke, wrote to a friend:

The "death squadron" strikes in so many poor homes. It is a daily thing—death and bodies found everywhere. . . . I am beginning to see death in a new way. For all these precious men, women, children struggling in just laying down their lives as victims, it is surely a passageway to life or, better, a change of life.

December 28, Holy Innocents

We remember today, O God, the slaughter of the holy innocents of Bethlehem by King Herod. Receive, we pray, into the arms of your mercy all innocent victims; and by your great might frustrate the designs of evil tyrants and establish your rule of justice, love, and peace.

—*Book of Common Prayer*

Scripture Readings

The scriptures speak about justice and peace constantly and in a multitude of ways. Here are a few of these texts that might be taken for prayer and reflection.

Genesis 8:6—9:17
Exodus 22:21–27
Deuteronomy 5:1–22;
   6:4–25
Job 31:16–32
Sirach 4:20–31
Isaiah 2:2–5; 26:1–6;
   32:16–20; 58:6–11
Jeremiah 8:15–22
Ezekiel 34:25–31
Joel 2:12–29
Amos 5:1–24
Jonah
Micah 6:8
Matthew 5:38–48
Luke 6:27–38
John 14:23–29
1 Corinthians 1:18–21
Ephesians 4:25—5:2
Philippians 4:4–9

Colossians 3:12–15
Hebrews 11:35—12:2
James 2:1–7; 3:13–18;
   4:1–10
1 Peter 3:13–18
Revelation 21:1–6

Among the many psalms that speak of justice and of peace are the following:

4, 5, 10, 17, 23, 34, 46, 72, 85, 122, 131, 133, 146.

PRAYERS

Our God, the Guide of humanity, let your spirit
rule this nation and its citizens, that their deeds may
be prompted by a love of justice and right, and bear
fruit in goodness and peace.

Bless our people with love of righteousness.

Teach us to work for the welfare of all, to diminish
the evils that beset us, and to enlarge our nation's
virtues.

Bless our people with civic courage.

Bless our striving to make real the dream of your
kingdom, when we shall put an end to the suffering
we now inflict upon each other.

Bless our people with a vision of your kingdom
on earth.

You have given us freedom to choose between good
and evil, life and death. May we choose life and good,
that our children may inherit from us the blessings
of dignity and freedom, prosperity and peace.

—*Gates of Prayer*

Holy Creator of the universe, of the earth and its people, you have allowed humanity to run astray in wholesale madness throughout history, wherefore nothing remains for us but to sink to our knees in tears before you who created us. Give us all the courage and valor to achieve peace and real disarmament. Give the Church the courage to teach not how one can cleverly reconcile the egotism among us, but rather how in light of the folly of the cross one can, and indeed must, assume direct responsibility for unconditional justice and peace. Convert the hearts of the mighty so that they may not yield to the deceitful pursuit of power in order to justify their own actions, nor deceive themselves and others while claiming to serve the ends of peace by proliferating arms. And ultimately: teach us within our own lives to further the cause of peace unselfishly.

—*Karl Rahner*

God of power and mercy,
you destroy war and put down earthly pride.
Banish violence from our midst
    and wipe away our tears
that we may all deserve to be called
    your sons and daughters.

—*Roman Missal*

Maker and lover of peace,
to know you is to live,
and to serve you is to reign.
All our faith is in your saving help;
protect us from people of violence
and keep us safe from weapons of hate.

—*Adapted from the Roman Missal*

Lord our God,
you have given all peoples one common origin,
and your will is to gather them
     as one family in yourself.
Fill the hearts of all with the fire of your love
and the desire to ensure justice
     for all their brothers and sisters.
By sharing the good things you give us
may we secure justice and equality
     of every human being,
an end to all division,
and a human society built on love and peace.

—*Adapted from the Roman Missal*

God grant me the serenity to accept the things
I cannot change, the courage to change the things
I can, and the wisdom to know the difference.

—*Serenity Prayer*

Lord, there are many such,
Dwelling in narrow resentments,
Embittered by wrongs that others have inflicted,
Drained of hope and bereft of peace,
Left to great hatred in this world.

Judge and turn their oppressors.
Release again, for the fearful,
The springs of trust and goodness.
Give them liberty of heart
The liberty of those who leave room
For the judgment of God.

Enlarge our hearts, O God,
That we may bear the sorrows of the weary,
And seek and serve thy will.
Great art thou, O Lord.
There is nought that is a match for thee. Amen.

—*Surah of Ṭā Hā, v. 26*

Mary, Queen of peace, we entrust our lives to you.
Shelter us from war, hatred and oppression. Teach
us to live in peace, to educate ourselves for peace.
Inspire us to act justly, to revere all God has made.
Root peace firmly in our hearts and in our world.

—*John Paul II*

SONGS

O day of peace that dimly shines
Through all our hopes and prayers and dreams,
Guide us to justice, truth and love;
Delivered from our selfish schemes.
May swords of hate fall from our hands,
Our hearts from envy find release,
Till by God's grace our warring world
Shall see Christ's promised reign of peace.

Then shall the wolf dwell with the lamb
Nor shall the fierce devour the small;
As beasts and cattle calmly graze,
A little child shall lead them all.
Then enemies shall learn to love,
All creatures find their true accord;
The hope of peace shall be fulfilled,
For all the earth shall know the Lord.

　　—Carl P. Daw, Jr.

Let there be light,
Let all the nations gather,
Let there be understanding,
Let them be face to face.

Open our lips,
Open our minds to ponder,
Open the door of concord
Opening into grace.

Perish the sword,
Perish the angry judgment,
Perish the bombs and hunger,
Perish the fight for gain.
Hallow our love,
Hallow the deaths of martyrs,
Hallow their holy freedom,
Hallowed be your name.

Your kingdom come,
Your spirit turn to language,
Your people speak together,
Your spirit never fade.

Let there be light,
Open our hearts to wonder,
Perish the way of terror,
Hallow the world God made.

—*Frances W. Davis*

For the healing of the nations,
Lord, we pray with one accord;
For a just and equal sharing
Of the things that earth affords.
To a life of love and action
Help us rise and pledge our word.

Lead us now, Lord, into freedom,
From despair your world release;
That redeemed from war and hatred,
All may come and go in peace.
Show us how through care and goodness
Fear will die and hope increase.

All that kills abundant living,
Let it from the earth be banned;
Pride of status, race or schooling,
Dogmas that obscure your plan.
In our common quest for justice
May we hallow life's brief span.

You, creator God, have written
Your great name on humankind;
For our growing in your likeness
Bring the life of Christ to mind:
That by our response and service
Earth its destiny may find.

—*Fred Kaan*

O God of ev'ry nation,
Of ev'ry race and land,
Redeem your whole creation
With your almighty hand;
Where hate and fear divide us
And bitter threats are hurled,
In love and mercy guide us
And heal our strife-torn world.

From search for wealth and power
And scorn of truth and right,
From trust in bombs that shower
Destruction through the night,
From pride of race and station
And blindness to your way,
Deliver ev'ry nation,
Eternal God, we pray.

Lord, strengthen all who labor
That we may find release
From fear of rattling saber,
From dread of war's increase;
When hope and courage falter,
Your still small voice be heard;
With faith that none can alter,
Uphold us by your word.

Keep bright in us the vision
Of days when wars shall cease,
When hatred and division
Give way to love and peace,
Till dawns the morning glorious
When Christ alone shall reign
And he shall rule victorious
O'er all the world's domain.

—*William W. Reid*

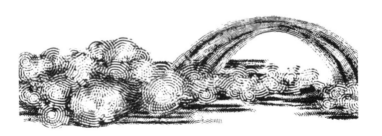

Great God, Your love has called us here
As we, by love, for love were made.
Your living likeness still we bear,
Though marred, dishonored, disobeyed.
We come, with all our heart and mind
Your call to hear, Your love to find.

We come with self-inflicted pains
Of broken trust and chosen wrong,
Half-free, half-bound by inner chains,
By social forces swept along,
By powers and systems close confined
Yet seeking hope for humankind.

Great God, in Christ you set us free
Your life to live, Your joy to share.
Give us Your Spirit's liberty
To turn from guilt and dull despair
And offer all that faith can do
While love is making all things new.

—*Brian Wren*

*Other songs include "I'm gonna lay down my sword
and shield" and "We shall overcome" with its verses:
"We'll walk hand in hand," "We are not afraid,"
"We shall live in peace" and "The Lord will see
us through."*

REFLECTIONS

We have sinned against life by failing to work for peace. We have sinned against life by keeping silent in the face of injustice. We have sinned against life by ignoring those who suffer in distant lands. We have sinned against life by forgetting the poor in our own midst. . . . Let now an Infinite Presence teach us a gentleness that transcends force and melts our hardness of heart.

—*Gates of Repentance*

If this task of building a peaceful world is the most important task of our time, it is also the most difficult. It will, in fact, require far more discipline, more sacrifice, more planning, more thought, more cooperation and more heroism than war ever demanded.

—*Thomas Merton*

The ultimate weakness of violence is that it is a descending spiral, begetting the very thing it seeks to destroy. . . . Returning violence for violence multiplies violence, adding deeper darkness to a night already devoid of stars. Darkness cannot drive out darkness; only light can do that. Hate cannot drive out hate; only love can do that.

—*Martin Luther King, Jr.*

On my knees I beg you to turn away from the paths of violence and return to the ways of peace. . . . Violence only delays the day of justice. Violence destroys the work of justice. . . . Do not follow any leaders who train you in the ways of inflicting death. . . . Love life, respect life, in yourself and in others. Give yourself to the service of life, not the work of death. . . . Violence is the enemy of justice. Only peace can lead the way to true justice.

—*John Paul II*

The bread in your cupboard belongs to the hungry; the coat hanging unused in your closet belongs to the one who needs it; the shoes rotting in your closet belong to someone who has no shoes; the money which you put in the bank belongs to the poor. You do wrong to everyone you could help but fail to help.

—*Saint Basil*

Shall I not tell you what is better than prayers and fasting and giving alms to the poor? It is making peace between one another: enmity and malice destroy all virtues.

—*Sa'id ibn al-Musayyab (Follower of Muhammed)*

On praying with open, outstretched hands: On one occasion I gained new insight into this ancient gesture, when I read somewhere that the Assyrians had a word for prayer which meant "to open the fist." The fist, and especially a fist raised threateningly, is a sign of a high-handed, even violent person. People grasp things in closed hands when they are unwilling to let go of them; they use clenched fists to assault and hurt and, even worse, to beat others down so that they cannot get up. Those who pray, however, are saying before God that they are renouncing all high-handedness, all pride in their own sufficiency, all violence. They open their fists. They hold up their empty hands to God: "I have nothing that I have not received from you, nothing that you have not placed in my empty hands. Therefore, I do not keep a frantic hold on anything you have given me; therefore, too, I desire not to strike and hurt but only to give and to spread happiness and joy. For I myself am dependent on God, who fills my empty hands with gifts."

—*Balthasar Fischer*

We Christians do not bear arms against any country;
we do not make war anymore. We have become
children of peace, and Jesus is our leader.

—*Origen, third century*

The arms race is to be condemned unreservedly. It
is an act of aggression which amounts to a crime,
for even when they are not used, by their cost alone,
armaments kill the poor by causing them to starve.

—*Statement of the Holy See, 1976*

Paperwork, cleaning the house, cooking the meals,
dealing with innumerable visitors who come all
through the day, answering the phone, keeping
patience and acting intelligently, which is to find
some meaning in all those encounters—these
things, too, are the works of peace, and often seem
like a very little way.

—*Dorothy Day*

War no more! War never again!

—*Paul VI at the United Nations, 1965*

An Order of Service for Peace

When people gather to pray for peace, the order
of service might be drawn from the Liturgy of the
Hours or the Liturgy of the Word. An evening
service can begin with the lighting of a candle and
continue with the burning of incense while a psalm
is sung. Or, it could begin with a call to prayer,
silent reflection and praying together, "I confess . . ."
Songs, at the beginning or at other times during
the service and at the end, can be taken from the
examples in this book. Opening and closing prayers,
if used, can be composed beforehand or chosen
from the prayers in this book.

   Scripture texts can be taken from those of the
Sunday or feast, or from the suggestions made on
page 35. After the scripture and after any spoken
reflection on the scripture (some of the texts that
begin on page 47 can be used if there is no homily),
there should be ample time for silence. In addition
to an appropriate psalm, the service could include
the singing or recitation of the Benedictus (in the
morning) or the Magnificat (in the evening). Partial
texts of these canticles are found here on page 3
and pages 6 and 7.

Prayers of intercession should be carefully prepared; other prayers can be added by the assembly, leading to the Lord's Prayer. At the end, the peace greeting can be exchanged among all those present.

Acknowledgments continued from page ii

Texts on pp. 1 and 7 are excerpts from the English translation of *Book of Blessings*, © 1988, ICEL. All rights reserved. Used with permission.

The selection from Psalm 104 is based upon Psalm 104 from the *New American Bible*, © 1970 Confraternity of Christian Doctrine, Washington, D.C. Used with permission.

The English translations of the gospel canticles (Song of Zachary, p. 3, and Song of Mary, pp. 6–7) have been prepared by the English Language Liturgical Consultation, Washington, D.C.

Texts on pp. 1, 7, 23, 26, 32: from *Catholic Household Blessings and Prayers*, © 1988, United States Catholic Conference, Inc., Washington, D.C. Reprinted with permission. All rights reserved.

Lord, make me, p. 21: from *Catholic Household Blessings and Prayers*.

Texts on pp. 10, 27 and 31: from *The Challenge of Peace, God's Promise and Our Response*. © 1988 United States Catholic Conference, Inc., Washington, D.C. Reprinted with permission. All rights reserved. Paragraphs 298, 302, 111 and 114. *Footnote to paragraph 111: Representative authors in the tradition of Christian pacifism and nonviolence include: R. Bainton, *Christian Attitudes Toward War and Peace* (Abington: 1960), chaps. 4, 5, 10; J. Yoder, *The Politics of Jesus* (Grand Rapids: 1972); *Nevertheless: Varieties of Religious Pacifism* (Scottsdale: 1971); T. Merton, *Faith and Violence: Christian Teaching and Christian Practice* (Notre Dame: 1968); G. Zahn, *War, Conscience and Dissent* (New York: 1967); E. Egan, "The Beatitudes: Works of Mercy and Pacifism," in T. Shannon, ed., *War or Peace: The Search for New Answers* (New York: 1980), pp. 169–187; J. Fahey, "The Catholic Church and the Arms Race," *Worldview* 22 (1979): 38–41; J. Douglass, *The Nonviolent Cross: A Theology of Revolution and Peace* (New York: 1966). *Footnote to paragraph 114: [Citation for final quote:] Sulpicius Severus, *The Life of Martin*, 4.3.

Texts on pp. 8–9, 18, 38 and 39, excerpts from the English translation of the *Roman Missal*, © 1973, International Committee on English in the Liturgy, Inc. (ICEL); text of prayer "Above the clamour," p. 12, from *Opening Prayers for Experimental Use at Mass* © 1986, ICEL. All rights reserved.

The human heart, p. 28: excerpt from the Holy Father's statement of September 12, 2001, published on the U.S. Catholic Bishops' website, www.nccbuscc.org.

We believe that, p. 29: joint statement issued September 14, 2001 and published on the U.S. Catholic Bishops' website, www.nccbuscc.org.

Be praised, p. 30: in *Francis and Clare, the Complete Works*, tr. Regis J. Armstrong and Ignatius C. Brady. New York: Paulist Press, 1982, pp. 38–39. © 1982 by The Missionary Society of St. Paul the Apostle in The State of New York, www.paulistpress.com.

Can there be, p. 33: in *The Long Loneliness, the Autobiography of Dorothy Day*, copyright 1952 by Harper & Row Publishers, Inc. Copyright renewed © 1980 by Tamar Teresa Hennessy. Reprinted by permission of HarperCollins Publishers Inc.

Holy Creator, p. 37: in *Prayers for a Lifetime*. Copyright © 1984. All rights reserved. Used with permission of The Crossroad Publishing Company, New York.

Songs

Yet with the woes, p. 15: the last two stanzas of "It came upon the midnight clear." Music can be found in many hymnals, including *Worship*, #400.

Again we keep, p. 16: can be found in many hymnals, including *Worship*, #420. It can be sung to other tunes, including "Praise God from whom all blessings flow."

Lord, there are, p. 40: trans. Kenneth Cragg, in *Alive to God, Muslim and Christian Prayer*, compiled by Kenneth Cragg. London: Oxford University Press, 1970, p. 117.

O day of peace, p. 41: Text: Carl P. Daw, Jr. © 1982 by Hope Publishing Co., Carol Stream IL 60188. All rights reserved. Used by permission. Can be found in many hymnals, including *Worship*, #654 and also can be sung to the tune for the *Magnificat*, *Worship*, #15. It may be sung to long meter tunes (making four stanzas), such as, "Creator of the stars of night," "The glory of these forty days" and "Praise God from whom all blessings flow."

Let there be light, p. 42: American Peace Society, Washington, D.C., can be found in *Worship*, #653.

For the healing of the nations, p. 43: © 1968, can be found in many hymnals, including *Worship,* #643. It can be sung to "Praise my soul, the king of heaven" (LAUDA ANIMA) and "Let all mortal flesh keep silence" (PICARDY).

O God of every nation, pp. 44–45: © 1958, renewed 1986, Hymn Society of America, Texas Christian University, Forth Worth, Texas. All rights reserved. Used with permission. It can be found in many hymnals, including *Worship,* #650 and also can be sung to "O Christ the great foundation" ("The church's one foundation," AURELIA), "All glory, laud and honor" (ST. THEODULPH), or "O sacred head surrounded" (PASSION CHORALE).

Great God, your love has called us here, p. 46: © 1977, Hope Publishing Company, Carol Stream, Illinois. All rights reserved. Used with permission. It can be sung to the tune of "Faith of our fathers" (St. Catherine) and may be found in *The Presbyterian Hymnal,* #353.

We have sinned, p. 47: in *Gates of Repentance: The New Union Prayerbook for the Days of Awe.* New York: Central Conference of American Rabbis, © 1978, 1996, pp. 404, 403.

If this task, p. 47: in *Faith and Violence, Christian Teaching and Christian Practice.* Notre Dame IN: University of Norte Dame Press, © 1968, p. 42. Used with permission.

The ultimate weakness, p. 48: in *Where Do We Go from Here? Chaos or Community?* New York: Harper & Row, 1967. © 1967 Martin Luther King, Jr., renewed 1995 Coretta Scott King. Reprinted by arrangement with The Heirs to the Estate of Martin Luther King, Jr., c/o Writers House, Inc. as agent for proprietor.

On my knees I beg you, p. 48: speech made in Ireland, 1979.

The bread, p. 49: Homily 6, On Avarice (on Luke 12:18).

Shall I not, p. 49: Malik ibn Anas, *Al-Muwatta',* 7th hadith in the Book of Good Character.

On praying with, p. 50: from *Signs, Words & Gestures,* trans. Matthew J. O'Connell. New York: Pueblo Publishing Co., p. 27.

We Christians, p. 51: *Origen Against Celsus,* V, 33.

Paperwork, p. 51: from *The Catholic Worker,* December 1965, 7. May be found on the Catholic Worker website: www.catholicworker.org.